Rushmoor Remembers

Aldershot, Farnborough and Cove in the First World War

Friends of the Aldershot Military Museum

2014

Contributing authors:

Roger Deason
Barbara Reese
Peter Reese
Melita Stone
Paul H. Vickers

Edited by Paul H. Vickers

Copyright © Friends of the Aldershot Military Museum, 2014.

All rights reserved. No part of this publication may be reproduced, stored in a retrieval system, or transmitted in any form or by any means, electronic, mechanical, photocopying, recording or otherwise, without the prior permission of the publishers.

ISBN 978-0-9566484-1-9

All proceeds from the sale of this book go to the Friends of the Aldershot Military Museum to support their work to preserve and promote the heritage of Aldershot's military town. The Friends of the Aldershot Military Museum are a registered charity, number 1108637.

CONTENTS

Acknowledgments	v
Chapter One: Aldershot goes to war	1
Chapter Two: The New Armies	12
Chapter Three: Treating the wounded	23
Chapter Four: Farnborough and aviation	29
Chapter Five: Life in the civilian towns	35
Chapter Six: Women in the war	47
Chapter Seven: The 1st/4th Battalion, the Hampshire Regiment	51
Chapter Eight: The end of the war	55
Chapter Nine: Memorials to the Fallen	59
Appendix: Aldershot Command in August 1914	63

ACKNOWLEDGEMENTS

This book is based on the research and material originally assembled by members of the Friends of the Aldershot Military Museum for the special exhibiiton "*Rushmoor Remembers: Aldershot, Farnborough and Cove in the First World War*" which was presented at the Museum from 6th August to 21st September 2014, to mark the centenary of the start of the First World War.

For their support towards the *Rushmoor Remembers* projects, the Friends of the Aldershot Military Museum gratefully acknowledge the grants from the Heritage Lottery Fund and Rushmoor Borough Council.

The Friends of the Aldershot Military Museum are grateful to the Curator, staff and volunteers of the Aldershot Military Museum for their assistance and co-operation. We are also indebted to the following institutions who have generously given assistance with facilities for research, loan of items for display, or made available photographs from their collections: Hampshire County Council Arts and Museums Service, Winchester; Farnborough Air Sciences Trust; Army Medical Services Museum, Mytchett; Royal Hampshire Regiment Museum, Winchester; and the Prince Consort's Library, Aldershot.

This book would not have been possible without the work of many volunteers. The Friends of the Aldershot Military Museum are grateful to the following who have researched the history or loaned material from their private collections: John Austin; Brian Ballard; Reg Davis; Roger Deason; Tim Down; George and Rita Farthing; Barbara Fletcher; Jo Gosney; Alan Grover; Peter Jenner; Peter and Barbara Reese; Alan Ryder; Peter Smith; Harold Smith; and Melita Stone.

Paul H Vickers
Editor

CHAPTER ONE

Aldershot goes to War

In 1914 Aldershot was the greatest single garrison in the country. The "Camp at Aldershot" had been founded in 1854 but had mainly been wooden huts, except for a line of brick barracks along its southern edge. In 1890-1895 the wooden huts were removed and brick barracks erected throughout the Camp. It was in these barracks that the soldiers of the resident formations lived.

The civilian town of Aldershot grew in tandem with the Army. A complete new town centre was built immediately south of the Camp in the last half of the nineteenth century. By the start of the twentieth century it was a thriving community with many shops, hotels, theatres, public houses, and the new innovation of the cinema. Similarly to the north of the Camp a new shopping and residential area was built in south Farnborough, today known as North Camp.

Aldershot Garrison had two resident infantry divisions, 1st Division in South Camp and 2nd Division in North Camp, plus the 1st Cavalry Brigade in South Camp. In August 1914 the Garrison comprised 3 regiments of cavalry, 13 battalions of infantry, 12 batteries of artillery, 5 companies of Royal Engineers, 22 companies of Army Service Corps, 6 companies of Royal Army Medical Corps, 2 companies of Ordnance Corps, plus supporting units including veterinary sections and military police. In all there were 17,643 soldiers in Aldershot.

It was also the centre of the wider Aldershot Command, which included Farnborough with 4 squadrons of the Royal Flying Corps, Bordon (4 infantry battalions, 6 artillery batteries), Blackdown (2 infantry battalions), Deepcut (6 artillery batteries), Pirbright (1 infantry battalion), Woking (1 infantry battalion), Ewshot (6 artillery batteries), Longmoor (3 Royal Engineers companies),

5th Dragoon Guards march up the High Street, Aldershot, returning from rifle training to Warburg Cavalry Barracks. The Westgate Centre and Princes Hall now occupy the site of Warburg Barracks.
(Photo courtesy of Peter Smith)

and detachments at Sandhurst and Camberley. Across Aldershot Command there was a total of 27,245 personnel. At this time the total British Army strength was 247,798, of whom about half were overseas across the Empire. Aldershot Command was home to around 20% of the home force, it was the largest Command in the UK and the position of General Officer Commanding, held by Lieutenant General Sir Douglas Haig since 1912, was the most prestigious home appointment.

The Royal Aircraft Factory
(Photo courtesy of Roger Deason)

Farnborough had quickly become established as the centre for aviation since Samuel Cody had made his first pioneering flight from Laffan's Plain in 1908. By 1912 the Royal Engineers Balloon Factory had grown into the Royal Aircraft Factory, the new Royal Flying Corps was formed in Farnborough, and the town became known as the home of many great air pioneers.

The general officer commanding was Lieutenant General Sir Douglas Haig, who had been GOC in Aldershot since 1912. On 29th July 1914, Haig received a Telegram from the War Office ordering that "Precautionary Measures" as detailed in the Defence Scheme should be put in place. Haig wrote that "All our arrangements were ready, even to the extent of having the telegrams written out. These merely had to be dated and despatched."[1] Under these measures warning telegrams were sent to reservists and to the Territorial Army, and all regular officers and men on leave were recalled and all further leave was cancelled, much to the annoyance of the soldiers, especially as 3rd August was a Bank Holiday. One officer of the 11th Hussars was on his honeymoon, which he had to cut short and return to Aldershot. Others were at a polo tournament at Goodwood, which also had to be abandoned.

Mobilisation Orders for Aldershot Command had been revised as recently as 2nd March. For some years mobilisation had been regularly practised, one of the Aldershot Divisions being "mobilised" at the expense of the other and joined by volunteers from the Reserve, so that it could take part in manoeuvres at full war establishment. A test mobilisation of the 2nd Division was carried out on 27th July 1914 and the "mobilised" Division was inspected by their commander, Major General Archibald Murray, on the 29th.

General mobilisation was ordered in France, Belgium and Germany on 1st August. At 12 noon that day the German ultimatum to Russia expired and the German declaration of war was delivered by its ambassador in St Petersburg at 7 pm. In Britain, on 2nd

August the government cancelled the planned annual training for the Territorial Army and the regular Army manoeuvres. The officers in Aldershot were now expecting the mobilisation order at any time. Captain Henry Dillon of the 2nd Oxfordshire and Buckinghamshire Light Infantry wrote in a letter to his uncle:

> This war has come so suddenly one hardly realises it - I expect they will get us, the two Aldershot divisions across within a few days ... I would strongly advise you to lay in a lot of provisions now as everything will be famine prices in no time and there will be crowds of starving people about. Personally I am so thankful that I shall be one of the first to go as if the war goes on for long it will be fearful at home. We have not actually started mobilizing but I expect we shall tomorrow.[2]

On the 3rd August Germany declared war on France, and on the morning of 4th German army units crossed into Belgium. The British ambassador in Germany was instructed to ask for his passport to leave the country if no satisfactory answer had been received by midnight (11 o'clock UK time) regarding British demands for Germany to observe Belgian neutrality.

At 5.30 pm that evening, at Government House, the GOC's official residence, General Haig received a telegram containing the one word "Mobilise" and signed "Troopers", which was the code name for the Secretary of State at the War Office. The Command Headquarters sent out the orders in turn to their subordinate HQs, and on to the individual units. At midnight on 4th August, Captain Harding-Newman telephoned from the Headquarters Office to Government House to inform Haig that the War Office had wired "War has broken out with Germany" and Haig was required to attend a Council of War at the War Office the next day. Haig wrote that the "orders were put in force and methodically acted upon without friction and without flurry. Everything had been so well thought out and foreseen that I, as 'C-in-C Aldershot', was never called upon for a decision."[3] Having sent on the orders, Haig went to bed.

The Government declared the 5th August as the first day of mobilisation. In 1914 the carefully worked-out timescale for mobilising an infantry battalion was three days. However, the Government had to recognise that the timing was unfortunate, not only because the 3rd August was a Bank Holiday but also because the lateness in issuing orders cancelling the annual Territorial Army training exercises meant that many personnel, reservists and units were in the wrong places and could not reach their mobilisation points according to the planned timetable. They decided on a short postponement and gave orders that embarkation would not begin earlier than the 9th August.

In Aldershot, the mobilisation of the resident units was quickly underway. It was at 6.30 p.m. on the 3rd August that a soldier had hoisted the mobilisation signal, three large black balls, to the top of the flagstaff on the lawn outside the HQ building in Stanhope Lines. Troops started vanishing from the streets, and it was noted that there were no soldiers in the second house in the Hippodrome that evening.

Lieutenant General Sir Douglas Haig

In August 1914, the General Officer Commanding in Aldershot was Lieutenant General Sir Douglas Haig.

Haig was born in Edinburgh on 19th June 1861, the son of a Scotch whisky distiller. After attending the Royal Military College, Sandhurst, Haig was commissioned into the 7th Hussars in 1885. He served under Kitchener in the Sudan (1898) and commanded a cavalry column in the later stages of the Boer War. Haig was posted to India as inspector-general of cavalry, served in the War Office from 1906–09, and was Chief of Staff of the Indian army. He was appointed GOC at Aldershot in 1912.

After mobilisation the Aldershot Command formed the bulk of 1st Corps, which spearheaded the British Expeditionary Force in France, and Haig was given its command. He left Aldershot in the evening of the 14th August, travelling by car to Southampton where he stayed overnight before sailing next day for France.

In 1915 Haig took command of the British 1st Army, and replaced General French as Commander-in-Chief of British forces in December that year. Haig ordered the attacks on German positions along the Somme in 1916, in which the Army sustained terrible losses. The following year the battles of Arras and Ypres also resulted in heavy loss of life, but despite criticism at home, notably from Lloyd George, Haig remained British Commander-in-Chief and was in command for the final victory in 1918.

In 1921, Haig helped found the British Legion, to improve the welfare of ex-servicemen and their families, and served as its first president. He was also chairman of the United Services Fund.

Douglas Haig remains a controversial figure to the present day.

Units issued the equipment their men needed for war. Detailed inspections of kit, weapons and, for the cavalry, saddlery, followed, and deficiencies were made good. Each man was issued with clothing, equipment, weapons, 100 rounds of ammunition, identity disc, a first aid field dressing, jack knife, and iron (or emergency) rations consisting of a tin of bully beef, six biscuits, some tea and sugar in a tin, and two tubes of meat extract. Owing to the huge numbers of reservists who needed to be equipped, it was decided to take one of the two pairs of boots which the regulars should have had, so that there were sufficient boots for the reservists as they were called back. As a result the soldiers who went to France did so with only one pair of boots, a shortage which was to have serious effects later on.

Regimental property, including Officers' and Sergeants' mess plate and furniture, was packed away and put into storage for the duration of the war. The 11th Hussars reported that their property was sent to White's, an Aldershot contractor, under the charge of the regimental Bandmaster. Public property which was not needed, such as full-dress uniforms and headgear, was returned to the Ordnance Department. Accounts and ledgers had to be closed, for which boards of audit were hastily convened.

The symbol for mobilisation, black balls raised to the top of the flagpole outside Aldershot Command Headquarters. This photograph was taken on 5th August 1914, the day after the declaration of war. (Photo courtesy of Paul Vickers)

Another essential was the collection and allocation of the extra horses which were required. The need for horses was part of the plans which had been put in place before the war, with a census taken of all horses in the country and statutory powers enacted to requisition all that were needed. Throughout Britain from the start of mobilisation some 120,000 horses were collected in 12 days, and animals poured into the Aldershot remount centre. They were of variable quality, some were hunters and fine animals, others had been out to grass and were not fully fit for war work. One Aldershot funeral director lost three horses to the Royal Artillery, the unfortunate battery that took them on was promptly nicknamed 'The Body Snatchers'.

The regiments' most precious items, the regimental colours, had to be laid away safely for the duration of the war. The colours of the 2nd Worcestershire Regiment were taken back to Worcester by special escort and handed to the care of the Dean and Chapter of the cathedral until the battalion would need them again. The 2nd Oxfordshire and Buckinghamshire Light Infantry sent their colours to the regimental depot at Cowley for safe keeping. The 2nd Highland Light Infantry found the time to send off their colours with an appropriate ceremony at which the colour party paraded in full dress for the last time.

With thousands of reservists coming into Aldershot to join their regiments, any army building that could be converted into sleeping accommodation was pressed into service with libraries, lecture halls and gymnasia amongst the buildings brought into use. Despite these measures, still more provision was needed and tented camps appeared on any open ground, while work began on building more permanent huts to be ready for the winter. The first Aldershot Command fatality of the war occurred on 5th August when 33 year old Corporal Arthur James Whittington of the Army Service Corps was erecting tents for the new arrivals. He felt unwell and laid down for a rest. When his colleagues tried to wake him later they found he was dead. Whittington was the first of 690 First World War casualties to be buried in the Aldershot Military Cemetery.

Amongst those under canvas were No. 20 Field Ambulance who mustered on Redan Hill in a line of bell tents, one of many medical units camped on this site. A bell tent could take 14 men and there were many reports of minor scuffles and bad language at night as a result of the overcrowding. For those who could not find a tent, nights were often spent sleeping on a blanket on the ground. W.T. Davies, of 42nd Field Ambulance, recorded spending his first night sleeping under a field ambulance wagon.

On the 6th August the *Aldershot News* reported a column of men "miles long" seen marching in the camp. A typical working day for the soldiers was reveille at 5.30, a route march, breakfast at 7.30, drill, demonstrations and lectures on subjects such as first aid or sanitation, followed by another route march and foot inspection with dinner at 13.00. After that it was odd jobs with many men all but off duty. Many soldiers visited the Cambridge Military Hospital for a typhus injection, although this was not compulsory. The emphasis on marching was intentional, with the object of hardening the men's feet as well as improving overall fitness.

Soldiers in Aldershot in 1914.   (Photo courtesy of Paul Vickers)

Troops march through Church Crookham. (Photo courtesy of Reg Davis)

Men were medically examined, recruits mustered, and the reservists, now flooding into Aldershot in large numbers, were united with their parent units. The reservists were needed to bring the units up to war establishment, and also to take the places of those soldiers who could not go to the front because they were under-age. Under the rules in place in 1914, no-one under twenty years of age could go on active service so, for example, the 1st Black Watch had to leave behind 200 men from their peacetime establishment. The Highland Light Infantry sent 300 fully clothed and equipped reservists to join their 2nd Battalion at Aldershot on 5th August, with 400 more following the next day to bring the battalion up to war strength. The War Diary of the 1st Scots Guards recorded that on the 5th August "Three parties of reservists arrived. Magnificent, clean, steady men."[4] Between the 6th and 8th August 599 reservists returned to the 2nd Oxfordshire and Buckinghamshire Light Infantry, and 485 men for the Royal Munster Fusiliers arrived on 7th August, as did 351 for the Connaught Rangers, to be followed by two more drafts of 236 and 48 in the next two days. Two batches of 100 men arrived for the 1st Loyal North Lancashire Regiment. Captain Arkwright of the 11th Hussars was sent from Aldershot to Dublin on 5th August to select the number of reservists required to bring the regiment up to strength, and he returned three days later with 120 men.

As the reservists arrived they were put through courses of drill, rifle and machine gun training, and, for the cavalry, riding and sword drill. The Colonel of the 5th Dragoon Guards had his own method of deciding which reservists were ready to join the regulars of his regiment. If a man was a first-class shot, his age and former service were not considered. Jumps were set up in the Riding School and the men were tasked to ride the course bare-backed. Those who got round the course were placed on the list of those to go to the front at once, after passing the medical examination and other formalities. Those who did not complete the jumps course were put back for further training.

Morale was generally high, especially among the younger officers who saw the war as embarking on a great adventure. However, some more senior officers took a more realistic view of what lay ahead. One night in the Officers' Mess of the 5th Dragoon Guards the subalterns were noisily expressing their enthusiasm until their commanding officer, Lieutenant Colonel Ansell, came down in his pyjamas "and told them in unmistakable terms that war was likely to prove very different from what they seemed to imagine".[5] When Brigadier Briggs, commanding 1st Cavalry Brigade, was asked what level of casualties he expected, he replied that commanding officers should expect to lose fifty percent of their regiments in the first week of fighting.[6]

The 1st Battalion Scots Guards was at full strength ready to move out by midnight 6th/7th August, the 1st Black Watch, 1st King's Regiment and the 2nd Oxfordshire and Buckinghamshire Light Infantry on the 8th, and the Highland Light Infantry on the 9th. At midnight on 7th/8th August, the 6th Brigade reported mobilisation complete, followed by the 5th Brigade at midnight 8th/9th August. The 11th Hussars was complete in men, equipment and horses by 11th August.

The 9th August was a Sunday and church parades were held as normal, except that the men wore service dress instead of the full dress which had been the custom in peacetime.

On 11th August King George V took the salute at a royal review of the Aldershot Command. The King and Queen arrived in Aldershot at 12 noon and were met by General Haig, who joined them in an open car as they toured the lines. After the review their majesties lunched with Haig and his wife. During the visit the King asked Haig what he thought of the appointment of Sir John French as Commander in Chief of the British Expeditionary Force. Haig did not believe French was the right man and had expressed his view at the War Office with some force, but he "thought it sufficient to tell the King that I had 'doubts' about the selection".[7]

The next day, 12th August, the first units left Aldershot for France. Unlike the departure for the Boer War there was no pomp and ceremony, soldiers just quietly left by train, usually in the early hours of the morning. When the 1st King's Regiment entrained at Farnborough at 6 am on the 12th August it was reported that "two or three porters, a few officers' wives and a sleepy paper boy were the only witnesses of their departure."[8] The only music seems to have been for the Highland Light Infantry who left their barracks at 3.30 am on 13th August and marched through the deserted streets of Aldershot with their pipers playing at the head of the column. To protect secrecy the soldiers were kept on a constant state of readiness but only given short notice of their departure date, leaving them 24 hours to complete packing and mobilising.

The *Aldershot Gazette and Military News* described the scenes of the departing units in its issue of 14th August 1914, under the headline "For King and country - Stirring scenes of patriotism at Aldershot":

> Au revoir! to all our soldiers who have left the Command for active service. A spirit of enthusiasm filled the heart of every officer, non-commissioned officer and man who departed from Aldershot the other morning. Dawn was fast gaining supremacy over the beautiful harvest moon. But there was sufficient light to recognise parting friends while the silence was so acute as to enable one to catch the faint sobs of women who stood near as their husbands left their parade …. Then suddenly the will o' the wisp like twinkling of a light, and a moment later the harsh and rasping blare of a bugle! It was the disturber of sleep - it was the long waited for signal for the moment for action! Lights sprang into being with wonderful rapidity, and soon came the pattering of many feet and the shouts of men … company upon company of men were falling in on parade. Women and not a few children seemed to flit around one, and tender good-byes were being uttered and many kisses given!. The stirring scene raised the lump in the throat more effectively than anything it had been the writer's lot to experience. The grim reality of all it meant made one a sharer of the enthusiasm and the seriousness … Marching off under sealed orders might have directly defined the situation, for no one beyond the officers knew the destination - only the knowledge that the railway station was the immediate rendezvous had leaked out amongst the men, every one of whom carried his complete fighting kit, and a means it was hoped sufficient to go a long way towards silencing the enemy.
>
> "Not good-bye, but au revoir," was an oft-spoken wish as hearty handgrips were given. May it prove so; may all those brave men return again. … And as they marched forward at the quiet and kindly command of their leaders many turned away with a prayer on their lips for their success and safety during the troublous times before them.

General Haig's wife wrote about the impact on the wives as the men mobilised:

> When the blow came it was very overwhelming, though work kept the wives from grieving too much; but I shall never forget myself the troops marching past Government House at dead of night … I want to make special mention of the bravery of the wives and mothers at that time. Amongst them one never heard one word of complaint. Of course the sorrow of parting had been too deep to talk about."[9]

The order of departure of the Aldershot units (where known) was:

12th August:

> 1st Division, 2nd Infantry Brigade, from Farnborough. 1st Loyal North Lancashire Regiment (2 trains, 1.15 and 2.15 pm)

2nd Division, 6th Infantry Brigade, from Farnborough. 1st King's (Liverpool) Regiment (8.00 am); 2nd South Staffordshire Regiment; 1st Royal Berkshire Regiment (2 trains, 10.27 and 11.30 am). Probably also 1st King's Royal Rifle Corps.

13th August:

1st Division, 1st Infantry Brigade, from Farnborough. 1st Coldstream Guards (overnight of 12-13 August); 1st Scots Guards (2 trains, second departed 6.25 am); 1st Black Watch; 2nd Royal Munster Fusiliers.

2nd Division, 5th Infantry Brigade, from Government Sidings. 2nd Worcestershire Regiment (2 trains, 7.00 and 8.00 am); 2nd Oxfordshire and Buckinghamshire Light Infantry (2 trains, 12.38 and 2.02 pm).

From Aldershot: 2nd Highland Light Infantry; 2nd Connaught Rangers (2 trains, 9.50 and 11.00 am).

RAMC No. 2 Field Hospital (2 trains).

14th August:

Haig left Aldershot in the evening, travelling by car to Southampton where he stayed overnight before sailing next day for France.

15th August:

Cavalry Brigade leaves - 5th Dragoon Guards from Farnborough Station in 4 trains from 5.15 am to 8.39 am, 11th Hussars from South Farnborough (North Camp) in 4

"Goodbye Daddy". Soldiers of the Royal Army Medical Corps depart from Government Sidings, Aldershot.. (Photo courtesy of Paul Vickers)

trains from 9.30 am to 10.40 am. Also 2nd Dragoon Guards, probably from Farnborough.

2nd Division Headquarters left Aldershot shortly after 6 am.

The first destination was Southampton, but for security even the train drivers were only told their route at the last moment. All civilian trains in and out of Aldershot had been suspended during the first days of the war to leave the track clear for military use, under legislation passed in 1871 which allowed the government to take control of the railways. This restriction was now extended with civilian trains banned from several locations between Aldershot and the South Coast as the Army headed for the channel ports.

From Southampton the units were ferried to France within 24 hours, landing at Le Havre and Boulogne, from where they moved into Belgium to meet the enemy.

The Black Watch leaves Aldershot.
(Photo courtesy of Peter Smith)

Notes
1. Sheffield, Gary and Bourne, John (eds). *Douglas Haig: War diaries and letters 1914-1918*. Weidenfeld and Nicolson, 2005, p. 52.
2. Harris, Simon. *History of the 43rd and 52nd (Oxfordshire and Buckinghamshire) Light Infantry in the Great War, 1914 - 1918*. Volume II. Rooke, 2012, p. 3.
3. Sheffield, Gary and Bourne, John, *Op. Cit.* p. 52.
4. Petre, F Loraine. *The Scots Guards in the Great War 1914-1918*. John Murray, 1925, p. 8.
5. Lumley, L R. *History of the Eleventh Hussars 1908-1934*. RUSI, 1936, p.22.
6. *Ibid.*
7. Sheffield, Gary and Bourne, John , *Op. Cit.* p. 56.

8. Wyrall, Edward. *The history of the King's Regiment (Liverpool) 1914-1919*. Volume I. Edward Arnold, p. 4.
9. Countess Haig: *The man I knew*. Moray Press, pp. 108-109.

CHAPTER TWO

The New Armies

On 6th August 1914 Parliament authorised the recruitment of 500,000 new soldiers. On the 28th another 100,000 were authorised with the age limit raised to 35, and another 500,000 were approved on the 15th September. When Lord Kitchener made his famous appeal for new recruits to come forward huge numbers responded. Aldershot, the country's greatest permanent army camp, was the reception point for thousands of the recruits over the next four years. Six new Divisions were formed and two of them were based at Aldershot Command. The area hosted 28 battalions, double the peacetime strength.

These men had just started to arrive when the regular soldiers of the 1st and 2nd Divisions left for France. With their departure, room was freed up in the Aldershot barracks, however the continuous influx of new recruits and reservists soon filled all available space. An order was issued that all barracks must be altered to increase sleeping capacity by 50 per cent. The Army Service Corps were particularly challenged when 1,500 newly enlisted labourers arrived in town needing somewhere to sleep. By the end of

Troops returning from training march down Grosvenor Road in 1914.
(Photo courtesy of Paul Vickers)

Recruits for the Scottish Division in Aldershot, 1914. These are men who responded to Kitchener's call for volunteers, parading in their civilian clothes as they have not yet been issued with uniforms. (Photo courtesy of the Aldershot Military Museum)

August a constant stream of troops was pouring into town, the new recruiting stations often sending men in batches of 100 at a time.

This was the biggest influx of recruits in British army history and the system struggled to cope with the numbers. Private John Jackson, from Glasgow, had volunteered in the Cameron Highlanders in 1914. He caught the train to "the great military centre of Aldershot", on a journey that took 21 hours. On arrival in Aldershot, he was

> marched off to the gymnasium in Maida Barracks, which was to be our temporary residence. This was the beginning of the roughest period of my experience as a soldier at home. We were each given a boiled potato (skin included) and a piece of meat for our dinner. We did not have plates, knives, or forks, nor yet tables to sit at. No, our tables were the floor-boards. Perhaps allowances should be made at this time, for the unpreparedness of the authori-ties, with regard to the abnormal numbers of recruits, but with all things considered it was sickening to men who had previously known decent home-life. We became more like animals than humans, and only by scrambling and fighting like dogs were we able to get food to eat. Some may read this and imagine that I exaggerate, but men who went to Aldershot in 1914 know I speak the truth. Our bedding was a solitary blanket, and our bed the block-paved floor of the gymnasium, so our training to withstand hard-ships began on arrival.[1]

It was not just accommodation which was in short supply, the recruits often had no uniforms or equipment. Private James Wilson of the 7th Leicestershire Regiment recalled:

We were sent to Aldershot, where we were quickly sorted out and began training the first day we arrived ... I was only a kid but a number of men in the battalion were real tough Yorkshire miners. We had no uniforms and our civilian shoes wore out before we ever received boots, in fact the miners said they would refuse to parade again if they didn't get proper boots. After a time we were given uniforms but not khaki, there was no khaki to be had, so they gave us a red uniform with navy blue cuffs and white braiding ... we didn't get khaki until March 1915.[2]

The 23rd Division were raised on 13th September in the Frensham area, and moved to Aldershot in December. With their civilian clothing rapidly being reduced to rags they welcomed the arrival of blue uniforms in October. The same month they received 100 out-of-date Lee Enfield rifles per battalion to practice drill and 400 sets of old buff equipment. In December old pattern water bottles and white haversacks were received. The 20th (Light) Division started to receive khaki in February 1915 and had to use a mixture of civilian, colonial, hunting and army horse tackle.

The shortages of uniforms and equipment did not stop the recruits from being given a full programme of training and the Army certainly kept them busy. A typical week would see 6 hours of physical drill, 10 hours of squad drill, 12 hours of musketry, 18

Cavalry training for the New Army. (Photo courtesy of Paul Vickers)

*Infantry recruits for the New Army in Stanhope Lines, Aldershot.
(Photo courtesy of Paul Vickers)*

hours of squad drill with arms - if arms were available - and 2 hours of "other work". Private Jackson gave his impressions of the Camp at this time:

> We found Aldershot to be a hive of soldiers in different stages of training. In addition to the various regular barracks, camps had been formed wherever space could be found. As a training centre it is splendidly situated, and fashioned on modern ideas and requirements. Each barracks is complete in itself, from its officers' and 'married' quarters, to a well appointed cook-house and general offices.
>
> Recreation grounds, then used for encampments, were every-where, also comfortable recreation rooms and reading rooms ...The different barracks were separated by splendidly kept drives, which were bordered by gardens and shrubberies.[3]

As the war went on, the number of enlistments started to fall off and it became clear that conscription was inevitable. The National Registration Act was passed in July 1915, aimed at stimulating recruitment and discovering how many men aged between 15 and 65 were engaged in each trade. All those in this age range, not already in the military, had to register. By August 1915, 19,000 had registered in Aldershot and 8,000 in Farnborough. Conscription was formally introduced in 1916 and the Military Services Act came into effect on 2nd March. Tribunals were set up in Aldershot and Farnborough to hear appeals against conscription on grounds of doing essential war work, ill health, domestic obligations, or conscientious objection. The scale of the call-up is shown in

Aldershot's Wartime Generals

Major General Sir A. H. Gordon. (Photo courtesy of Aldershot Military Museum)

After Haig was appointed to command 1st Corps, the post of General Officer Commanding (GOC) in Aldershot passed to Major General Sir Alexander Hamilton Gordon. He had joined the Royal Artillery in 1880 and served in the Afghan War (1880) and the South African War (1899-1901). Gordon was Deputy Assistant Quartermaster General in Aldershot from 1901-1904, and at the outbreak of the First World War was Director of Military Operations in India. In May 1916 Haig appointed Gordon to command 9th Corps in France, a position he held until September 1918. Gordon was followed at Aldershot by General Sir Archibald Hunter.

Hunter was commissioned in 1875 and had served in the Gordon relief expedition (1885), was awarded the DSO for action against the Mahdists, and had been with Kitchener in the 1896–8 operations which recaptured Khartoum. Hunter was at the battle of Omdurman (1898) and served in the South African War. In August 1914 he was appointed commander of the Aldershot Training Centre, responsible for training men for the New Armies, and in January 1917 was made GOC Aldershot Command. He repeatedly requested a command in France but was too old for a front-line command. In September 1917 Hunter when he was made Aide-de-Camp General to the King. His replacement as GOC was General Sir Archibald Murray.

Murray had entered the army in 1879. In the South African War he was awarded the DSO for leading an attack in the northern Transvaal. Before the First World War Murray held a series of staff appointments, including senior General Staff Officer of the 1st Division at Aldershot. In World War One he was appointed Chief of the General Staff of the BEF by Sir John French, under whom he had served at Aldershot. In February 1915 Murray became Deputy Chief of the Imperial General Staff responsible for superintending the training of the New Army. In December 1915 he was sent to command in Egypt. Replaced by Allenby in 1917, Murray returned to Britain as GOC Aldershot and remained in that post until 1919.

General Sir A. Murray. (Photo courtesy of Aldershot Military Museum)

Cove. In January 1918 the *Aldershot News* reported that more than 200 residents out of a population of just 1,750 were currently under arms and that just about every man fit for service was in the forces.

In August 1917 members of the Women's Auxiliary Army Corps were stationed in Aldershot. They were marched down to the station with the band leading them cheerfully playing "There's a girl for every soldier".

The Coffee Room in the Church of England Soldiers and Sailors Institute in Victoria Road, Aldershot. (Photo courtesy of Peter Smith)

During the war soldiers' homes and institutes had a vital role in maintaining morale. Existing institutes included Miss Daniell's Soldiers' Home in Barrack Road, Church of England Institutes in Victoria Road and in North Camp, the Roman Catholic Soldiers' Club in Knollys Road, the Primitive Methodist Home in Victoria Road, Wesleyan Soldiers' Homes in Grosvenor Road and in North Camp, and the Methodist Soldiers' Home in Smith-Dorrien House. Two new homes were opened during the war, the St Andrew's Scottish Soldiers Club in May 1916 in Mandora Road, and in July 1916 the Percy Illingworth Institute on Gun Hill, funded by the Baptists. The importance of these institutions was reflected by Private John Jackson, who wrote in 1914:

> A well known building in Aldershot was the 'Smith-Dorrien' Soldiers' Home, which contained a billiard-room, reading and writing rooms and a good library. In it were also a post-office, private baths, and a buffet ... The 'Home' was always crowded when men were off duty, and many thousands of men will have pleasant recollections of happy evenings at the Smith-Dorrien Home.

Smith-Dorrien House refreshment room. (Photo courtesy of Paul Vickers)

The Primitive Methodist Soldiers' Institute in Victoria Road, Aldershot, in November 1917. Institute staff are seated in front, with some of the many soldiers who used the institute. (Photo courtesy of Peter Smith)

Charles Rumble

Charles Rumble was born in Redhill in 1870. He served as a Sergeant in the Northamptonshire Regiment, and although he had left the regular Army he was recalled for service in the South African War from 1899-1901.

After the war he worked at the Soldiers' Home in Pirbright, which had been run by his wife during the South African War. Charles then became Area Manager for the Methodist Soldiers' Homes, and during the First World War he worked tirelessly at the Smith-Dorrien Home in Aldershot. His work was of major importance for soldiers' welfare and morale, and the soldiers were greatly appreciative of all he did for them.

Charles continued his work through the Second World War, assisted by his daughter.

Charles Rumble pictured at his house 'Rozel' in Mytchett with his grandchildren and one of their friends.
(Photo courtesy of Tim Down)

In November 1914 the East End School was opened in the evening for soldiers to write home, read newspapers, enjoy entertainment and take refreshments. The teachers worked there voluntarily after the school day to assist the soldiers.

The Billiard Room of the All Saints Church Rooms and Institute, which was in Talavera Barracks, adjoining Hospital Hill, Aldershot. (Photo courtesy of Peter Smith)

Queen Alexandra paid for a soldiers' recreational hut in Hospital Hill, opened in March 1915. The Alexandra Hut was run by the YMCA, who also converted the old Masonic building in Station Road into a soldiers' club which opened in April 1916. In September 1916 the YMCA bought the Farnborough Conservative Club for use as a soldiers' home, and in February 1917 they took over the Hale Institute for soldiers based at Hungry Hill. The Salvation Army opened a recreation hut on Gun Hill in April 1917.

In 1915 the Farnborough Town Hall was taken over as accommodation and a club for the Royal Flying Corps. In South Farnborough, the Soldiers' Rest Rooms were used mainly by men from the RFC and from Blackdown Camp.

When the Women's Auxiliary Army Corps arrived in Aldershot in 1917, the YWCA in Union Street was opened for them. Meals were served on the ground floor, while the first floor was for reading and writing and it had a small library.

In September 1917 the Army converted a canteen in Corunna Barracks into the Stanhope Concert Hall, to provide shows for the soldiers. In 1918 bi-weekly concerts were also held at the Parish Hall for wounded soldiers, and the Palace Cinema provided free entertainment for wounded servicemen.

Notes

1. Jackson, John. *Private 12768:memoir of a Tommy*. Tempus, 2004, pp16-17.

2. Van Emden, Richard. *Britain's last Tommies: Final memories from soldiers of the 1914-18 War in their own words*. Pen and Sword, p. 51.

3. Jackson, John. *Op.Cit*. p. 18

Prisoners of War

The main prisoner of war camp locally was at Frith Hill, outside Frimley. Later another camp was set up at Cove.

The Frith Hill Prisoner of War camp was opened in September 1914. In the early days of the war detainees were held in modified barracks. Frith Hill was one of the first 'permanent' camps, under the command of Major F. S. Picot of the Wiltshire Regiment, who had previously run a military detention barracks. There were two camps, one military and one civilian, each holding around 2,800 men. The Times described the arrival of some of the first German prisoners on 13th September 1914:

> "Uhlans with riding breeches and spiked helmets, infantrymen in uniforms of blue-green, sailors in navy blue and civilians in the garb in which they had been arrested - one with a white waistcoat which he had been wearing at a wedding party when taken."

Prisoners usually arrived at Frimley Station and were marched to Frith Hill, although occasionally they would come via Farnborough.

The civilian camp was used for interned aliens. Among the first groups in September 1914 were civilians from Bristol, Shrewsbury and Manchester. Adolphus Charles, the organist at the Garrison Church of All Saints, was interned in October when it was found that he was a German and had failed to register as an alien. In May 1915 400 London aliens arrived, who cheerfully sang 'Tipperary' as they marched into detention, followed by 300 the next day.

On 2nd September 1915 three men escaped from Frith Hill. Two were re-captured quickly, however Airman Ernest Junght stayed at liberty overnight leading to Aldershot being closely watched until his recapture. On 25th September 1916, five German prisoners escaped from a working party that had left Frith Hill for the day. Three were arrested two days later sleeping rough near Ascot.

There were also escape attempts from Cove. On 22nd August 1917 prisoner A. Nanjock escaped from the Camp, but he was recaptured a week later on the railway line at Hook. On Monday 8th October 1917 a gale struck the area and three PoWs used it as cover to escape. The escapers were two sailors and a soldier, named George Pauchstadt, B. Marten and E. Kilof. They were spotted in Camberley by the Frimley Urban District Council Clerk. He kept them under observation from his bicycle until he found a group of Cadets from Sandhurst, who detained the escapers. They were taken to Camberley Police Station and sent back to Cove on the 12 o'clock bus.

No Germans managed to escape from Britain during World War One.

The camp at Frith Hill, near Frimley, for German prisoners of war.
(Photo courtesy of Roger Deason)

German prisoners of war march from Frimley station to the camp at Frith Hill.
(Photo courtesy of Paul Vickers)

CHAPTER THREE

Treating the Wounded

Late at night on 30th August 1914 the first hospital train arrived at the Government Sidings, bringing around 200 wounded men from the battle of Mons. The soldiers were transferred to the two great Aldershot military hospitals, the Cambridge and the Connaught. Aldershot was the first place in Britain to take wounded troops from the Western Front, and a great many more would follow throughout the war.

The Cambridge Military Hospital in South Camp, Aldershot

During the summer of 1914. with the growing likelihood of war, preparations had been made for medical services for the British Expeditionary Force, both on the battlefields and at home. These involved the recruitment and training of staff, both medical professionals (doctors and nurses) and ancillaries. At Aldershot the Cambridge Military Hospital was mobilised on the 5th August 1914 and on the 13th August two

On the Western Front a horse-drawn ambulance passes a British tank. (Photo courtesy of the Army Medical Services Museum)

Ward No. 3 of the Cambridge Military Hospital, showing nursing staff and patients wearing the 'Hospital Blues' uniform. (Photo courtesy of Paul Vickers)

trains carrying equipment and personnel for the BEF departed from Aldershot Railway Station.

In France a chain of casualty evacuation was established, which began with Regimental Aid Posts near the front line from where ambulances, both horse-drawn and mechanical, transported the wounded to Field Hospitals then onwards to Base Hospitals near the coast and, if necessary, back to England.

In Hampshire further medical provision was provided by the British Red Cross in more than 60 hospitals and convalescent homes, many of them local to Aldershot and Farnborough. These establishments were overseen by the Royal Army Medical Corps and included Minley Hospital (where 1,829 patients were treated during the war), the Thurlston Hospital in Fleet, the Western House Hospital in Odiham and the Yateley Hospital (which treated 1,147 patients). In Frimley, The

The Connaught Military Hospital in North Camp, Aldershot. (Photo courtesy of Paul Vickers)

Empress Eugenie with staff and patients at Farnborough Hill.
(Photo courtesy of Jo Gosney)

Priory was offered to the Red Cross by Lady Gallwey and it opened in November 1915 with 40 beds, acting as an auxiliary to the Cambridge.

Empress Eugenie gave a wing of Farnborough Hill to be converted into a hospital for wounded officers, while the Abbot of Farnborough Abbey made Farnborough Court available for the duration of the war and 2,075 military patients were cared for, with the monks administering nursing as well as spiritual care. The use of Farnborough Court Hospital by Belgian troops saw a small Belgian population established in Farnborough. Much work was done by local volunteers helping the Red Cross at the War Hospital Depot. They also liaised with the Ministry of Food for the supply of food to the hospitals.

The Cambridge became the first British Military Hospital to have a dedicated Plastic Surgery Unit under the outstanding surgeon Harold Gillies. He was soon joined by William Kelsey-Fry, a dental surgeon, and together they pioneered maxillo-facial reconstruction. They were joined by the surgeon turned war artist Henry Tonks who graphically recorded pre and post-operative portraits of many patients. At the Connaught Hospital, in addition to the more obvious battle casualties, those suffering from shellshock and other mental conditions were also treated.

During the First World War the hospitals of Aldershot and Farnborough played an enormous part in the treatment and rehabilitation of thousands of Military personnel.

Sir Harold Gillies

*Harold Gilles.
(Photo courtesy of the Army Medical Services Museum)*

Harold Gillies was born in New Zealand in 1882, the youngest of eight children, and came to Britain in 1901. After attending Cambridge University he qualified as a doctor and worked at St. Bartholomew's Hospital.

At the outbreak of World War One Gillies joined the British Red Cross and in France observed the work of Claude Auguste Valadier, becoming fascinated with his restorative techniques. He went to Paris where he worked with Hippolyte Morestin who was also doing plastic surgery. So enthusiastic was Gillies about this work that he approached the chief army surgeon, Sir Arbuthnot-Lane, suggesting that a unit be set up in Aldershot as so many men were being admitted with hideously disfiguring wounds to their faces. The Army agreed to this, Gillies was made a Captain in the RAMC, and the Plastic Surgery Unit was opened at the Cambridge Military Hospital in July 1916.

At Aldershot Gillies and Kelsey-Fry worked together on the pioneering work of reconstructing the faces and jaws of disfigured soldiers.

With the Battle of the Somme, Gillies was warned there would be a major influx of patients and was allocated an extra 200 beds but it soon became clear that there was a need for even more space. Subsequently the unit moved to the Queen's Hospital in Sidcup. The work continued until the end of World War One and, between the units at Aldershot and Sidcup, Harold Gillies and William Kelsey-Fry reconstructed the faces of 11,572 patients.

Gillies was knighted in 1930. He died in 1960.

*Two of Gillies' patients, Pte Nash (top) and L/Cpl Bailey (above), drawn by Henry Tonks.
(Pictures courtesy of the Army Medical Services Museum)*

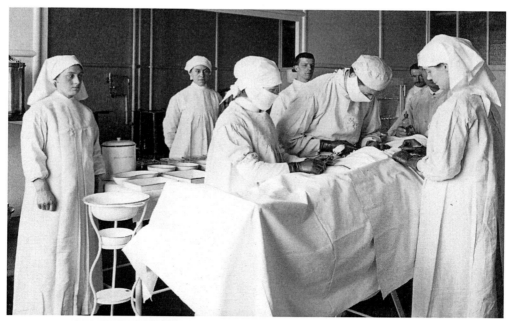

Above:

A hospital operating theatre in the First World War.
(Photo courtesy of the Army Medical Services Museum)

Left:

Soldiers from the Royal Army Medical Corps photographed outside McGrigor Barracks, Aldershot, which were built for staff of the Cambridge Military Hospital.
(Photo courtesy of Paul Vickers)

Group of wounded soldiers outside the Connaught Hospital.
(Photo courtesy of Paul Vickers)

The Connaught Hospital Recreation Hut.
(Photo courtesy of Paul Vickers)

CHAPTER FOUR

Farnborough and Aviation

In 1914, Farnborough was the national centre for aviation, home to the Royal Aircraft Factory and the headquarters of the Royal Flying Corps. The Royal Aircraft Factory had been created in 1911 from the Army Aircraft Factory, which had in turn developed from the Royal Engineers Balloon Factory. This had originally been in Gibraltar Barracks in Aldershot Garrison, but had moved to Farnborough in 1905 where there was space for it to expand. In 1914 the superintendent of the Royal Aircraft Factory was Mervyn O'Gorman, who had introduced scientific methods for aeronautical research and development. Among the significant developments at Farnborough had been the design and building of the Factory's first aeroplanes, the SE1 and BE1, which by 1914 had developed into the SE4 and BE2.

Farnborough was the base for the Royal Flying Corps. This was a relatively new corps, having been formally constituted by Royal Warrant on the 13th April 1912. Numbers 1, 2 and 3 Squadrons were formed at Farnborough on the 13th May 1912, Number 4 in September 1912 and Number 5 in August 1913. The Royal Flying Corps headquarters was in Building G1 adjacent to the airfield and is now the home of Farnborough Air Sciences Trust (FAST) Museum. It was originally built in 1907 by the Royal Engineers

The headquarters of the Royal Flying Corps. The building is now the Museum of the Farnborough Air Sciences Trust. (Photo courtesy of Peter Reese)

RFC planes at Farnborough: 5 Henry Farnam craft in the foreground; 5 BEs on the right, and Maurice Farnam planes in the rear. (Photo courtesy of Roger Deason)

to be the headquarters of their Balloon School and it is one of the oldest aviation related buildings in the country.

At the outbreak of war virtually every plane that was airworthy was sent to France to help make up four barely serviceable squadrons in support of the British Expeditionary Force there. The initial movement of the Royal Flying Corps Expeditionary Force to France was organised by Sir Frederick Sykes, who was replaced as Commandant of the Royal Flying Corps Military Wing by a 41 year old Major Hugh Trenchard (later Marshal of the Royal Air Force Sir Hugh Trenchard).

Trenchard arrived in Farnborough on 7th August 1914 and he related how, with everyone away, when he arrived he found his equipment was reduced to a battered typewriter, a

BE aeroplane with 60 HP Renault engine at Farnborough. The BE planes were designed and built at the Royal Aircraft Factory. (Photo courtesy of Paul Vickers)

confidential box and a safe. The box was found to contain shoes rather than military plans. On opening the safe he found a pair of well worn boots, together with Mess Bills of officers serving in France which they had undertaken to pay by the end of the war.

Under Trenchard activity quickened and he set about recruiting and training to replace losses in France and form new squadrons. On 7th October 1914 an RFC squadron flew to Belgium and by the end of the month five more squadrons were forming. These had been doubled to ten squadrons before Trenchard left for France on 18th November.

BE biplane no. 449 at Farnborough. (Photo courtesy of Paul Vickers)

Farnborough came to act as (Southern) Aircraft Repair Depot and by the end of the war it had received large numbers of aircraft such as DH4s, DH9s, DH10s, SE5s, and Dolphin and Martinsyde F3s, to be restored.

The adjacent Royal Aircraft Factory also saw a massive extension of its activities and new buildings were erected. Although official policy was for aircraft to be built by

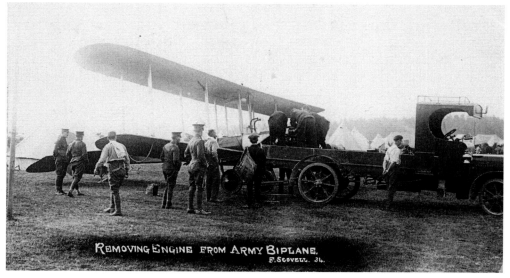

Staff from the Royal Aircraft Factory removing an engine from an Army biplane, watched by members of the Royal Flying Corps. (Photo courtesy of Peter Reese)

Major Frank Goodden

Frank Widenham Goodden was one of the key personnel at the Royal Aircraft Factory, Farnborough, where he flew the prototypes of the Factory planes and was Chief Investigator into aircraft accidents.

As a youngster Goodden used to watch the aviation pioneer A.V. Roe experimenting with planes on Lea Marshes. Goodden built his own plane in Oxford, although it never flew. He was involved in flying dirigibles, in association with airship designer Ernest Willows, and was also involved in the first ever British parachute jump from an airplane. The parachutist, William Newell, was in a seat on the wing of the plane and seemed reluctant to jump. Frank walked along the wing and pushed him off. Newell landed safely and history was made. Goodden performed the first ever loop the loop at night. He fixed a generator in the rear seat of his two-seater plane and lights along its body to ensure witnesses could see him perform the stunt.

In the years before the First World War, Goodden worked at various aviation schools. He joined the Royal Aircraft Factory as a civilian pilot on 7th August 1914, and was commissioned into the Royal Flying Corps in February 1915. In July 1915 he survived an aircrash at Shoreham, in which his passenger Henry Liley, a civilian tester with the Royal Aircraft Factory, was killed. In January 1916 Goodden was appointed Head of the Experimental Flying Department, and in October was promoted to Major and made a Squadron Commander.

Major Frank Goodden was killed in a plane crash on 28th January 1917.

private firms on sub-contract, it produced some 24 Handley Page 0/400 bombers and 2 Vickers Vimy aircraft, and before the armistice more than 400 aircraft of 30 different types had been made there. Along with construction work, which included 600 portable hangers, the Royal Aircraft Factory was engaged in the testing of aircraft, engines and other in-flight equipment for which large wind tunnels were built in 1917.

In February 1914 there were 957 employees at the Factory, but this grew rapidly druing the war. In 1916 the workforce reached its high point of over 5,000, over half of whom were women. Unsurprisingly, its scientists and other employees needed local accommodation. A new housing estate was built for them at Cove by prisoners of war, while other houses

Woman machinist at the Royal Aircraft Factory. (Photo courtesy of Farnborough Air Sciences Trust)

Group photograph of the women workers at the Royal Aircraft Factory, Farnborough. During the First World War about half of the workers were women and they played a vital role in enabling Farnborough carry out its essential work to support the Royal Flying Corps and Royal Air Force. (Photo courtesy of Farnborough Air Sciences Trust)

were erected just outside the factory in rows known as Pinehurst Cottages, and in North Camp in an area known as "Squares". In April 1918 the Royal Naval Air Service and Royal Flying Corps merged to form The Royal Air Force. The Royal Aircraft Factory was re-named the Royal Aircraft Establishment to avoid confusion between two RAFs.

While during the First World War Aldershot proudly stood as the largest concentration of military units and training facilities in Britain, Farnborough became synonymous with service aviation and the activities of its Royal Aircraft Establishment.

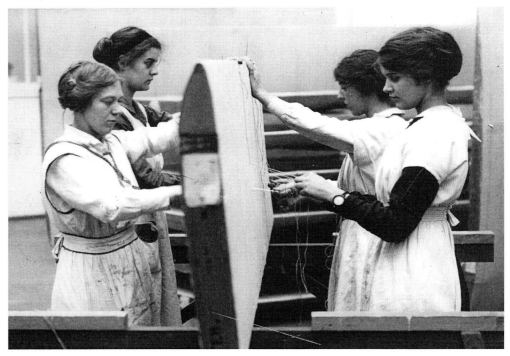

Women workers at the Royal Aircraft Factory stitching fabric onto a wooden frame to make the wing of an aeroplane. (Photo courtesy of Farnborough Air Sciences Trust)

CHAPTER FIVE

Life in the Civilian Towns

In the early days of the war local traders were struggling, owing to a combination of military orders and panic buying by the local people. This started in the days before mobilisation, partly as a result of dramatic food price rises, but it soon stopped. Traders also suffered from the government requisitioning horses fit for military use.

Aldershot Post Office worked around the clock from 29th July 1914, mainly due to telegraph work and when war was declared it opened for business 24 hours a day, in particular paying mobilisation cash orders. In a normal pre-war day around 150 telegrams would have passed through Aldershot, now it was nearer 1,500 with postmen and 3rd Aldershot Boy Scouts drafted in to help the messenger boys. Even the Labour Exchange was busy, arranging 800 civilian employees for the Army in just two days. To ease the Army workload, the Labour Exchange agreed to deal with their wages.

The staff of Aldershot Post Office in 1915.
(Photo courtesy of Peter Smith)

On 8th August 1914 Parliament approved The Defence of the Realm Act (known as DORA). This gave the authorities extensive powers to prosecute anyone found to be passing information to the enemy, and to secure all means of communication, railways, docks and harbours. DORA subsequently allowed the issuing of numerous new regulations which impacted on many details of life.

To keep order in the town military piquets, similar to Military Police, patrolled the streets throughout the day and night, and Aldershot and District Traction Company tried to get permission to appoint six Special Constables to protect their petrol store. This was refused as it was thought that the Police could do the job, but it was the first sign of a growing fear of spies and infiltrators.

With military piquets all over town, the locals quickly learned to pass by without seeming to pay too much attention to military activities. This message was reinforced when a prominent local JP found himself under arrest for seemingly paying too much attention to soldiers entraining at the station. After persuading the authorities that he was a respectable train spotter he was released.

Tragically the fear of enemy agents was to have fatal consequences for Jim Carroll, who was well known locally as he was the son-in-law of aviation pioneer Samuel F. Cody. On 20th August 1914 Carroll was out walking and stopped by the railway bridge at Boxalls Lane to chat with a sentry from the London Rifle Brigade. The soldier thought Carroll was suspicious but allowed him to continue down the path towards Badshot Lea. However Private Calfe, another sentry standing on the railway bridge, challenged Carroll. As he was deaf and had poor sight, Carroll did not respond despite several challenges. Calfe then fired one shot, which hit Carroll in the back. Carroll was taken to the Cambridge Military Hospital but died around midnight. This was probably the first civilian death at the hands of a nervous sentry in the war, and representatives of the War Department were present at the inquest to try and learn lessons to prevent similar occurrences.

One unexpected consequence of the war was seen at St Michael's Abbey in Farnborough where most of the monks returned to France to enlist in the French army. They were accompanied by Father Robo from Farnham.

An early casualty of the war was an attempt to form a 'town football team'. A public meeting had been arranged for the very week war was declared, but unsurprisingly the idea was dropped and Aldershot FC were not founded until 1926. Even so, on 31st August 1914, Aldershot Football Association met at the Royal Hotel and decided they would try to run all the planned competitions in the forthcoming season. This was

Aldershot Police, regular and special, 1914-1919, photographed outside the Police Station in the High Street. (Photo courtesy of Peter Smith)

Aldershot Fire Brigade, 1st January 1917. (Photo courtesy of Peter Smith)

highly controversial as football had already been criticised for playing on at a time of national crisis, and it compared badly with the Rugby Football Union's efforts to assist the war effort. To avoid criticism, Aldershot Football Association said they would write to the Army and offer to arrange football leagues and cups for the new recruits flooding into town. This fell by the wayside as the Army wrote back pointing out that the soldiers were fully occupied from 6 a.m. to 8 p.m. and had no time to play football. In September 1914 the Hampshire League suspended all further matches.

Aldershot and district suffered severe accommodation problems throughout the war. Adding to the military population were a great many wives and friends visiting soldiers in the barracks or in local hospitals. By 1915 people were knocking on random doors asking for a place to sleep, and often ended up sleeping rough. In 1915 Mrs. Tetley of Farnham paid for the refurbishment of the "Tin Hall" as a hostel for soldiers' wives and families, and allowed her own house to be used as a home for the sick and wounded.

In September 1917 a number of refugees from the bombing campaign in London started to arrive in the area. There were pitiable scenes as they walked the streets looking for lodgings. The Soldiers' Institutes allowed people to sleep on their floors, as did some civilians. In Frimley there were so many sleeping rough that the police asked shop keepers to allow people to sleep on their floors.

Fear of air raids meant that from October 1915 lights had to be put out at 8 p.m. (9 p.m. on Friday and Saturday). Aldershot Council also launched a campaign to recruit 92 auxiliary firemen, and a First Aid Corps was established.

William and Frank Smith

William Smith was a military tailor in Aldershot, with a shop at 185 High Street. His son, Frank Smith, was born in 1898 and worked as a driver for the Junior Army and Navy Stores, Union Street, Aldershot, from 14th June 1915.

On the 16th February 1917 Frank enlisted in the Army and joined the Army Service Corps. After a short time he was transferred to the Durham Light Infantry and served in Italy. Frank Smith was discharged on 6th December 1919.

Above: Military tailor William Smith, with his wife Rosetta.

Left: Private Frank Smith (on right) with fellow soldiers in the Army Service Corps

Below: "Op It!", a patriotic cartoon given in lieu of payment by a customer to military tailor William Smith of Aldershot.
(Photos courtesy of Harold Smith)

To tackle excessive drinking, Aldershot pubs were closed between 2.00 and 6.00 p.m. and at 9.00 p.m., a significant reduction from before the war when pubs often opened 15 hours a day. From February 1916 it also became an offence to buy a drink for another person. In 1915 there was a big temperance campaign with meetings in local churches and soldiers' institutes, where those attending were asked to sign pledges not to drink for the duration of the war.

The many voluntary efforts during the war included sending food parcels to prisoners of war, aid for the hospitals, and even a Russian flag day. The Iron Room, behind the Post Office in North Farnborough, gave wool to women knitting mittens and mufflers for the troops. In a tremendous effort during March 1918, from a population of only 40,000 Aldershot raised £104,000 in five days to buy a submarine.

Women collecting for the Russian Flag Day in Aldershot, October 1915. (Photo courtesy of Peter Smith)

In the last years of the war the Spanish Flu epidemic struck the area. The first cases were in autumn 1917 and by June 1918 the hospitals were full. School attendances declined, and on 29th October all schools were closed for a fortnight for disinfection. On that day one school had a 67% absence rate, including an entire class absent. The Traction Company regularly sprayed their buses down with formaldehyde and gave their staff Oxo or Bovril twice a day. Most deaths occurred at the Connaught Military Hospital, where soldiers suffering from the disease were taken. Influenza remained a potent threat beyond the end of the war.

An Empire Day certificate presented to 10 year old Harry Ballard, for his help in sending comforts to the troops. (Courtesy of Brian Ballard)

The Woolley Family

Members of the Woolley family, in a photograph dated 18th December 1917. Left to right:

Assistant Paymaster Herbert George Arthur Woolley, Royal Navy. Herbert had been commissioned as Assistant Paymaster on 15th July 1917.

Major Henry Copping, Royal Army Medical Corps. Henry Copping was born in 1842, joined the Army in 1860 and was commissioned in the Army Hospital Corps in 1879. He served in the Sudan during 1884-85 and retired in 1893. He was re-employed for the South African War (1899-1901) in the honorary rank of Major. He was re-employed again during the First World War, and granted the honorary rank of Lieutenant Colonel. At the time of the photograph Henry Copping was 75 years old. The Copping family was related by marriage to the Woolley family.

Assistant Adminstrator Miss M. Woolley, Women's Auxiliary Army Corps.

Mrs Woolley

Deputy Administrator Miss K. Woolley, Women's Auxiliary Army Corps.

Major Henry Woolley, Quartermaster, Royal Army Medical Corps. Henry was born in 1864 and served 14 years as a soldier and 4 years as a Warrant Officer before being commissioned into the Royal Army Medical Corps in 1899. He was promoted to Major on 13th December 1914.

Cadet S. C. Woolley, Dover College Officer Training Corps.

Billetting

The huge numbers of recruits which poured into Aldershot caused severe accommodation problems. As the 1914 winter approached many men in Kitchener's Army were still under canvas, so in November soldiers began to be billeted in private houses, starting with men from the Royal Army Medical Corps in the East End of Aldershot. In total about 3,000 men were billeted in Aldershot.

"How many can you take?"

Billeting was intended to be a short term solution while Army huts were constructed. However, in February 1915 problems with soldiers' housing continued and Newport Road School was closed for billeting. By the end of the month nearly all the schools were used for billets and remained closed until spring when the troops could return to tents. More men, mainly from the artillery, were billeted in the Park Estate, Grosvenor Road area, Alexandra Road, York Road, Waterloo Road and Holly Road. The Queen's Road Council Schools were closed for billeting for some of November and December 1915. On the outskirts, householders in Hale found themselves accommodating Army Service Corps soldiers as Alma Lane Camp was full. In January 1916 the West End schools were taken over by the Royal Flying Corps and the pupils sent to the East End School.

Initially Farnborough saw no billeting, as most of the houses in the area were already too over-crowded. However, from late 1915 the schools became billets with the pupils split between St Mark's Rooms, First Primitive Classroom and North Farnborough Council Infants School. The Town Hall and St Mark's Church Room were also commandeered, although the Town Hall rapidly returned to being a Soldiers Club.

Householders were compensated for taking in soldiers. In 1914 the daily rate was 2s 6d per man, which rose to 3s 4½d on 1st February 1915. For that the household was expected to provide bed and full board. In April 1915 the rates were reduced, as the policy had been in use longer than expected and was proving too costly.

Throughout the war the area suffered acute accommodation problems, not only for soldiers and families in Aldershot but also for workers at the Royal Aircraft Factory in Farnborough.

The Ballard Family

The photograph (right) shows the Ballard family in 1916. Standing left is Telegraphist David Ballard, and on the right his older brother Louis, both serving in the Royal Navy. Seated are his parents, his father wearing his South Africa War Medals. His mother wears an armband with the Ordnance badge, indicating that she was doing war work, probably in the Field Stores in Aldershot Garrison.

David Ballard enlisted in the Royal Navy in 1914 as a boy seaman, at the minimum age of 15½. He trained as a Telegraphist and progressed through the grades. Two years later he was aboard the battleship *HMS Neptune* at the great naval Battle of Jutland, where one of his friends, Boy Cornwall, earned a posthumous VC aboard *HMS Chester*.

After World War One he served aboard numerous other ships until his was discharged in 1939. However, David was recalled for service in World War Two and ended his 31 years service in September 1945.

Left: HMS Neptune, in which Leading Telegraphist David Ballard served at the Battle of Jutland
(Photos courtesy of Brian Ballard)

Food and Rationing

The war quickly pushed up prices locally. By September 1916 food prices had risen 65%, with sugar worst affected, rising 163%. A lack of coal deliveries meant there was "practically a coal famine" and petrol was rationed from August 1916. People caught "black-marketeering", or using children as "go-betweens" to get food from the Camp, faced heavy penalties. Several local traders were convicted of selling underweight bread, meat and sweets containing lead.

To help alleviate the problems of a lack of basic foodstuffs, in early 1917 the Council compulsorily took over 9 sites for allotments, including land on Ash Road, Church Hill and between St George's and St Michael's Roads. Similar moves followed in Farnborough and Ash, where Shawfield Recreation Ground was ploughed up. In April more land was taken over, including a plot on the corner of Station Road East and St George's Road, with much of Manor Park following. Within land owned by Aldershot Command, 321 acres were under cultivation by soldiers, and a further 364 acres of Government land were used for growing food.

In February 1917 there was an appeal for 'voluntary rationing', but nationally imposed restrictions soon followed. Local Food Control Committees were created to enforce the food control orders, which set out what types of food could be sold and the maximum prices allowed. Food hoarding was banned.

Shortages of butter and margarine during the pre-Christmas period of 1917 were exacerbated by people from outside coming to Aldershot knowing that the Army presence meant there was a good chance of supplies arriving. As a result local registration was imposed to buy butter or margarine, while children had priority for milk supplies.

The Aldershot Food Economy Committee opened a 'communal kitchen' on 21st March 1918, on the corner of Redan Hill and High Street. The kitchen cooked in bulk and sold at break-even prices, so reducing food wastage and helping working mothers feed their families. Around 300 meals a day were served. A second kitchen was opened in Queen's Road. The success of the Aldershot Kitchen led to calls for a similar initiative in Farnborough, but Farnborough Council said that no site was suitable.

Meat shortages caused Aldershot butchers to close on Mondays, Wednesdays and Fridays, and meat rationing was imposed locally on 7th April 1918. In an effort to increase the meat supply, in May 1918 Aldershot Council set up a piggery with around 12 pigs.

Despite the end of the war, meat rationing continued into 1919, although there was good news at Christmas with double rations issued. Butter came off rationing in early 1920, sugar in November.

A Board of Trade report found that between June 1914 and June 1918 the cost of living for an unskilled workman's family rose by 81%. Unfortunately food inflation would again become a serious problem in the immediate aftermath of the war.

A certificate of thanks given to a local boy for helping to send Christmas gifts to men in the Forces, 1916. (Courtesy of Harold Smith)

Examples of the many different designs of pottery items which were issued for the First World War, all with the Aldershot crest. (Courtesy of Barbara Fletcher)

The Farthing Brothers

Photo courtesy of George and Rita Farthing

This photograph shows the seven brothers of the Farthing family in 1917, when they were all serving in the War. They are (left to right):

Sergeant Charles Farthing, Army Service Corps

Warrant Officer Class 2 Tom Farthing, Army Service Corps

Sergeant Harry Farthing, 3rd (Toronto Regiment) Battalion, Canadian Expeditionary Force. Harry was living in St. Catherine, Ontario, in 1914, and enlisted in the 98th Battalion, later transferring to the 3rd (Toronto) Battalion. After the war he returned to his home town and settled in Aldershot.

Sapper Fred Farthing, Royal Engineers. On his sleeve he is wearing a long service stripe. After the war he emigrated to Canada.

Private George Farthing, 6th Dragoon Guards. George wears 5 long service and good conduct stripes, which indicates he has 23 years of service.

Corporal Bert Farthing, Royal Garrison Artillery. After the war Bert emigrated to Canada with his brother Fred.

Aircraftman Bill Farthing, Royal Flying Corps. William (Bill) Farthing had a long career in public service, and was Mayor of Aldershot from 1970-71, and Mayor of Rushmoor from 1977-78. William Farthing Close in Aldershot is named in his honour.

Bombardier Richard Ryder

Richard Chapple Ryder was typical of the many young men who served in the Army in the First World War. He was born in September 1896 and enlisted in the Royal Field Artillery on the 14th September 1915, aged 19. In Aldershot he was with 'B' Battery, 109th Brigade, RFA.

Bombardier Ryder (circled) in B Battery, 109 Bde RFA, Aldershot, 1916

In May 1916 Ryder went to France with his Battery. His time in action was short, for on the 1st June 1916 he was wounded at Le Bizet. Bombardier Ryder had injuries to his right arm, right lung and right leg. After treatment at the clearing station he was sent to the military hospital in Boulogne.

On the 30th June 1916 Ryder underwent an operation which removed a rib and took out pieces of shrapnel from his right arm. He had empyema, a build-up of fluid in the lungs, which was treated by the insertion of a drainage tube. His condition was described as "dangerous". In July Richard was sent to the Brook War Hospital in Woolwich. He underwent another operation in January 1917 for the empyema, and after another seven weeks he was able to get out of bed for the first time simce being wounded.

Richard Ryder wearing 'Hospital Blues', sketched by a fellow patient in military hospital.
(Courtesy of Alan Ryder)

On the 15th June 1917, Ryder was discharged from hopital and from the Army, as being "no longer physically fit for war service". He was aged 20 years and 9 months.

Unfortunately he was to suffer from his war injuries for many years, and had his right leg amputated in April 1920. Richard Ryder was in receipt of a disability pension from the time of his discharge from the Army.

CHAPTER SIX

Women in the War

Before 1914 all women, no matter their social status, suffered from inequality and disenfranchisement in a male-dominated society. For working class women life was a continual toil in unhealthy accommodation while scraping together enough money to survive. One third of all women did some paid work, but options were limited and, where no factory work was available, many became domestic servants. In the case of the better-off working and middle classes, women took clerical, teaching and nursing jobs. In both Aldershot and Farnborough enterprising women owned their own businesses, but were still only 10% of the business community. Even for the higher educated women from better off middle class families, the professional careers, such as law and banking, remained closed to them.

As the men enlisted, many women were faced with a considerable drop in income. Billeting of soldiers brought in some money, and a few designated women in the town were permitted to do laundry for the Camp. They were allowed to wash clothes for forty soldiers with no charge for water, but a Mrs Broadwood was fined 30 shillings for washing for 335 soldiers and exceeding her water allowance.

Gradually women moved into what was previously considered "men's work". The Aldershot Traction Company employed its first female bus conductor in November 1915. Miss K. A. Perrow became Aldershot's first Postwoman, at first just given a postman's badge in lieu of uniform. She was joined by Miss Bartlett in Farnborough and Miss M. Smith in Tongham.

In Farnborough the Royal Aircraft Factory employed a great number of women as clerical workers and factory hands, working alongside civilian men and servicemen. The first female casualty of the war at the Factory was Lily Veness, aged

Aldershot's first woman bus conductor, November 1915. (Photo courtesy of the Aldershot Military Museum)

21, who died of suspected poisoning from the dope painted on aircraft wings.

Dr Edythe Lindsay was the only female doctor in Aldershot during the war years, practising in Victoria Road. She was one of the first generation of female medical doctors and was a prominent local Suffragist. Dr Lindsay appears to be the only civilian who battled with the Council Authorities to set up a much needed VD clinic, which was not attained in Aldershot until 1916. It was estimated by a Royal Commission of 1916 that over 10% of the general population was infected with this disease, and not until then did it come into the public domain as a serious health issue

Among the more privileged, Lady Gallwey hired a local theatre to raise funds for the anticipated VAD

Miss Bartlett, Farnborough's first postwoman. (Photo courtesy of Jo Gosney)

Women working in a drawing office at the Royal Aircraft Factory, Farnborough. (Photo courtesy of Farnborough Air Sciences Trust)

*Working on wing frames at the Royal Aircraft Factory.
(Photo courtesy of Farnborough Air Sciences Trust)*

hospital, Lady Hunter helped with new facilities at the YMCA, and Mrs. Robie Uniacke, chairwoman of the Aldershot National Union of Women's Suffrage Societies, set up the Women's Wartime Club in St. Michael's Road. Rose Alexander of Aldershot Manor worked tirelessly to raise funds for the Aldershot War Hospital Supply Depot and was awarded the OBE for her efforts.

Many women supported charities sending food parcels and clothing to men at the Front, and at the Connaught Hospital some 60 women assembled splints and swabs.

The huge number of soldiers in the military camp attracted an increasing number of prostitutes. The problem was exacerbated when the Military cleared

Telephone staff, Headquarters Military Exchange, Aldershot, 1917. (Photo courtesy of Peter Smith)

the camp of all women, families included, into the civilian towns without providing any accommodation. Many charitable women rallied to help such distressed families. Mrs Maries, at the Presbyterian School Rooms, was very active in seeking out accommodation for soldiers families and those visiting the wounded in the hospitals. However, the all male Council issued prejudicial statements about "women's behaviour" and the Magistrates Court imposed heavy fines and prison sentences on those women who were brought before them for "inappropriate behaviour" or simply without a roof over their heads and unemployed.

By the end of the war the ratio of women in the workforce had risen to 46.75%, yet by 1921 it was back to pre-war levels of 25.4%. At the Royal Aircraft Establishment unskilled female staff were laid off, causing much distress at loss of income, and many who had found independence had to return to the confines of domestic service. Women who had joined the services were discharged with a week's pay. Employers now turned away women in favour of soldiers returning from the War.

In 1918 many, but not all, women gained the vote. However, the majority of women found the war years doubly hard. Nothing could assuage their deep feelings of bereavement for the loss of sons, husbands and fathers. With their close links to the Army, the women of Aldershot, Farnborough and Cove were especially aware, at first hand, of the sacrifices made.

Women did all types of work at the Royal Aircraft Factory. Most of the clerks in this huge office are women. (Photo courtesy of the Farnborough Air Sciences Trust)

CHAPTER SEVEN

The 1st/4th Battalion, The Hampshire Regiment

The territorials were at their annual exercises on Salisbury Plain when the mobilisation order was issued. The Hampshire Brigade Company of the Army Service Corps returned home and mobilised at Redan Hill Drill Hall. 'E' Company of the 1st/4th Hampshire Regiment, under Captain Hugh Foster, became the first British territorials to be deployed in the war. When the war broke out one of Aldershot's resident battalions, the Royal Munster Fusiliers, had been guarding the Royal Aircraft Factory but in August 1914 they were mobilised for service in France, so the local territorials relieved them. 'E' Company remained on duty until 29th August when they were relieved by London territorials. They returned to Salisbury Plain, not for exercises but to prepare for war.

In Aldershot a recruiting office specifically for the 1st/4th Hampshire Regiment was opened at the Aldershot Traction Company Depot in Halimote Road. Locally the battalion was nicknamed "Aldershot's Own".

In October 1914 the 1st/4th Hampshire Regiment departed for India, from where they deployed to Mesopotamia (modern day Iraq) in March 1915 to fight against the Ottoman Turks. The Battalion arrived in Basra on 14th March. By the end of July a combination of casualties from fighting and sickness, caused by the extreme conditions, had reduced the Battalion to less than 150 men.

Men of the 1st/4th Hampshire Regiment march to Arah Barracks, Dinapore, India, 14th November 1914. (Photo courtesy of the Royal Hampshire Regiment Museum, Winchester)

After being reinforced, the Battalion was ordered to Kut al Amara, where the British forces were gathering after a failed advance on Baghdad. The 1st/4th HQ staff and 'A' Company were in Kut when it was besieged by the Turks. Other companies who joined the forces attempting to relieve the siege suffered heavy casualties. Their numbers were so reduced that they were joined by the 5th Buffs, who had also suffered badly, to create a combined unit which was nicknamed "The Huffs". On 29th April 1916 the British forces in Kut surrendered, after suffering terrible conditions. 2,850 British and 9,000 Indian troops were captured, including 10 officers and 157 other ranks from the 1st/4th Hampshires. They endured a series of forced marches to POW camps, were

The 1st/4th Battalion of the Hampshire Regiment enter Baghdad, 13th March 1917. (Photo courtesy of the Royal Hampshire Regiment Museum, Winchester)

maltreated and underfed, and those who survived were put to work on the Constantinople to Baghdad railway. Of the British captives, only 750 survived to be repatriated after the war. These included all 10 officers of the 1st/4th, but less than 50 of the NCOs and privates.

The "Huffs" were disbanded in June 1916 and the 1st/4th was independent again. After a number of engagements throughout the rest of 1916 and into 1917, the British succeeded in taking Baghdad which the 1st/4th Hampshires entered on 13th March 1917.

In 1918 elements of the 1st/4th were sent into Persia (modern day Iran). Attached to 'Dunsterforce', they were sent to the Caucasus, between the Black Sea and the Caspian Sea, where Turkey bordered Russia. Following the Russian revolution this area was potentially open to attack from the Turks or Germans. During the campaign the 1st/4th were involved in repulsing an attack on Resht, the occupation of Baku, protection of the Trans-Caspian railway, and repulsing Bolshevik attacks.

Demobilisation did not begin until 1919, when men released on compassionate grounds departed in February. The main demobilisation began in March but proceeded slowly. The last cadre left for Bombay on 28th November 1919 and were back in the UK in December.

Captain James H. Harris

Captain James Harris was with the 1st/4th Battalion, Hampshire Regiment, and was taken prisoner after the siege of Kut. He was initially imprisoned in the Changi Camp, from where the prisoners were marched 60 miles in 4 days to Angora. Another march of 120 miles in 8 days brought Harris to the Yozgad prisoner of war camp on 24th April 1918.

On the night of 7th/8th August 1918 eight officers, including Harris, escaped from the camp and began a long walk south to the Mediterranean coast, which they reached on 30th August. It was a few days before they were able to steal a small motor boat on the night of 11th/12th September, and set out on a 120 mile journey to Cyprus, where they landed on the 13th September. After four days on the island they set off for Britain, arriving back home on 16th October 1918.

The escapers were Lieutenant Commander A. D. Cochrane RN, commander of HM Submarine H7; Captain A. B. Haig, 24th Punjabis; Captain R. A. P. Grant, 112th Infantry, Indian Army; Captain V. S. Clark, 2nd Royal West Kent Regiment; Captain J. H. Harris, 1st/4th Hampshire Regiment; Captain M. A. B. Johnston, Royal Garrison Artillery; Captain K. D. Yearsley, Royal Engineers; Captain F. R. Ellis, Duke of Cornwall's Light Infantry.

Captains Johnston and Yearsley wrote the story of the escape in the book "*450 miles to freedom*" published in 1919.

The escapers, photographed in Famagusta, Cyprus. Left to right: Captains Harris, Ellis, Haig, Lt Cdr Cochrane, Captains Clarke and Johnston. Seated: Captains Grant and Yearsley.
(Photo courtesy of the Royal Hampshire Regiment Museum, Winchester)

The survivors of Kut assembled at Winchester on 20th February 1919. Of the men of the 1st/4th captured at Kut, only around 40 survived. They are shown in this photograph, and include Aldershot men Sergeant Hedgman and Private T. W. Gullis. The men marched through the town, along streets lined by cheering crowds, and were given a civic reception at Winchester Guildhall and a lunch hosted by the Mayor. The menu, drawn up by Captain James Harris, was:

    Mule Tail Soup
    Roast (4th) Hampshire Hog
    Steak and kidney Pie (Busra flavour)
    Kut grass, roots, etc.
    Plum pudding and Tigris Water sauce
    Mespot jelly, Yesac blancmange
    Yallah cheese

(Photo courtesy of the Royal Hampshire Regiment Museum, Winchester)

CHAPTER EIGHT

The End of the War

On the morning of 11th November 1918 rumours swept through Aldershot that a ceasefire had been signed. The first sign that the story was true was when cheering and singing was heard from the Army camp. Crowds gathered in Aldershot town centre, whilst troops congregated in large numbers at the Army Headquarters. At 11.00 the Town Clerk was notified by Army HQ that a ceasefire had just come into effect and the Camp sirens were sounded. The people of the town realised the rumours were true and more flooded onto the streets. At the Army HQ General Murray appeared on the balcony, but few heard his speech for the cheering. A military band then led the soldiers around the parade ground, singing popular songs as they went.

Work came to a halt for the day. By 2.00 p.m. the town centre was thronged with people singing, dancing and waving flags, while more flags appeared on buildings. The schools joined in, singing the national anthem and patriotic songs before taking a half day off.

An unofficial march was led by the Army Gymnastic Staff, followed by the Guards, American Troops, Boy Scouts and anyone else who wanted to join in. Light rain was

no deterrent to the rejoicing. The Wellington Works' siren sounded for ten minutes along with church bells, the railway fog signal and railway engine whistles joining in a cacophony of noise not heard for many years. Several delivery vans were stripped of their goods, alcohol and cakes in particular. A Service of Thanksgiving was quickly arranged for the Municipal Gardens in the afternoon.

At night fireworks were set off, whilst the Camp loosed off Very lights, star shells and signal rockets. It was described as "the most delirious outburst of happiness ever, the most amazing scenes that Aldershot has ever witnessed".

On Wednesday 13th the Aldershot Volunteers continued the celebrations when their meeting at the Drill Hall quickly turned into a concert and ended with the men marching around town, cheering as they passed the houses of any of their comrades. On the 15th Farnborough hosted its first ever carnival. The brainchild of RAE employees, it brought out large crowds and raised a lot of money for charity. Employees brought mock ups of a tank with "Hang D.O.R.A" painted on it, a huge barrel on wheels marked "Government beer", two submarines, an airship, a German tank and a plane, HMS Victory, and finally Britannia showing off a caged Kaiser.

It was such a success that the whole event was staged again in Aldershot on the 30th. The parade around town culminated with a fireworks display at the Recreation Ground. The models of the Kaiser, a German airship, submarine and plane all ended up on the bonfire. The crowd enjoyed it so much that the other models followed, and only HMS Victory and a fire engine provided by Wrecclesham Boy Scouts survived.

Aldershot Fire Station, decorated in celebration of the peace.
(Photo courtesy of Paul Vickers)

SPECIAL ORDER OF THE DAY
BY FIELD-MARSHAL SIR DOUGLAS HAIG
K.T. G.C.B. G.C.V.O. K.C.I.E.
Commander-in-Chief British Armies in France

After more than four years of war, the enemy has been forced to ask for an armistice and has accepted the terms dictated by the Allies. Hostilities have been suspended and we may look forward to the early conclusion of a just and honourable peace.

At the moment of the definite triumph of those principles of liberty and right for which we entered the war, I desire to thank all ranks of all services of the British Armies under my command for the noble share they have taken in bringing about this great and glorious result.

My thanks are due to the officers, non-commissioned officers and men of the fighting forces (including the R.A.F.) who have served under my command in the prolonged struggle which has worn down and broken the strength of our opponents. Winter and summer the fierce strain has never ceased, has never for a moment been relaxed. Long and trying periods of trench fighting, countless raids and minor operations have bridged the gaps between the great battles on the Somme, at Arras, Messines, Ypres, Cambrai, and finally the tremendous conflicts of the present year, now crowned by victory.

In action you have been magnificent, equal to all changes of fortune, facing all dangers and surmounting all difficulties, your gallantry never failing, your courage most resolute, your devotion to duty unquestioning. Out of action, your time has been devoted, with a cheerfulness and energy undiminished by dangers and hardships undergone, to constant training and to the effort to make yourselves still more efficient. On such occasions your consistent good conduct and soldier-like behaviour have won for the British Army the esteem and lasting goodwill of the Allied peoples amongst whom you have lived.

To the non-combatant and auxiliary services, including the many thousands of women who by devoted work in so many capacities have assisted in the victory of our arms, I desire to express my deep gratitude for the essential service you have rendered.

No General has been given more loyal and whole-earted support by all ranks of the Commanders, Staffs, Departments and Services under him. No General ever yet commanded an Army of which he had greater reason to be proud.

By your efforts and those of the gallant armies of our Allies, the nations of the world have been saved from a great danger. You have fought for the sanctity of your homes, and for the liberties of those who will come after you. Generations of free peoples, both of your own race and of all countries, will thank you for what you have done.

We do not forget those who have fallen, and by their sacrifice have made our triumph possible. The memory of those who fought in the early battles of the war, few indeed in number but unconquerable in spirit, and the thought of all the brave men who have since died, live in our hearts to-day.

Our task is not yet finished, though the end is in sight. Until such time as the terms of armistice have been complied with and the conclusion of peace allows us to return once more to our homes, I rely confidently upon you to maintain on all occasions the same high standard of discipline, efficiency and good conduct which has always distinguished the British Army

General Headquarters,
13th November, 1918.

Commander in Chief
British Armies in France.

Field Marshal Sir Douglas Haig's Special Order of the Day after the Armistice had ended the fighting. (Courtesy of Harold Smith)

Captain A. Maurice Toye, VC, MC

Alfred Maurice Toye was born on 7th April 1897 at 'D' Terrace, Stanhope Lines, and was educated at the Aldershot Garrison School. At the start of the First World War he was serving with the Royal Engineers, until commissioned into the Middlesex Regiment in 1917, winning the Military Cross during the fighting for Passchendaele.

On the 21st March 1918, Captain Toye's 'C' Company was assigned to the defence of the bridgehead at Eterpigny, on the River Somme. After taking heavy casualties, Toye's company withdrew to the village which was then surrounded by the Germans. Toye was ordered to hold out, but he took the initiative and broke out with one officer and six men. He found 70 men of the Durham Light Infantry who were retiring, rallied them and led a counter-attack which was so effective that the whole German advance in the Eterpigny sector was checked. When relieved, 'C' Company was reduced to only 10 men.

Captain A. Maurice Toye, VC, MC (Photo courtesy of the Prince Consort's Library, Aldershot)

In the days that followed Toye led a group of personnel through an occupied village under heavy enemy fire. Despite being wounded twice, he charged the enemy, firing rapidly. This heroic act led his men out of danger. On 1st April Toye led a mixed unit in the recapture of a defensive line which had been abandoned just before his arrival.

Captain Toye was awarded the Victoria Cross for "most conspicuous bravery and fine leadership displayed in extremely critical circumstances." Toye was invested with the VC by King George V on 8th June 1918 in a ceremony on Queen's Parade, Aldershot. Captain Toye is the only holder of the Victoria Cross to have been born and raised in Aldershot.

After the war he served in North Russia, with the Rhine Army, and at the Royal Egyptian Military College. At the start of World War Two he was Commandant of the School of Chemical Warfare and later taught at the Staff College, before serving with the 6th Airborne Division in 1943-44. After World War Two he was promoted to Brigadier and retired from the Army in 1949 to become Commandant of the Home Office Civil Defence School. Illness forced him to retire and he died at Tiverton, Devon, in 1955 aged 58.

CHAPTER NINE

Memorials to the Fallen

The oldest First World War memorial in Aldershot is the 1st Division Cross, a wooden cross constructed by 23 Field Company Royal Engineers in 1916 on the battlefield of High Wood, in memory of the men from 1st Division who died in the Battle of the Somme. In 1927 the cross was brought to Aldershot and erected outside 1st Division Headquarters in Pennefather's Road. In January 1939, 23 Company RE reconstructed the south entrance of the Royal Garrison Church and moved the cross into the porch, where it is protected from the weather and still stands to this day.

The memorial to the soldiers of the 2nd Division stands at the junction of Hospital Hill and Knollys Road. It was designed by Captain J. B. Scott MC, an officer of the 2nd Division, and unveiled on 1st December 1923 by General Lord Home. The Reverend

Dedication of the 1st Division Memorial on 3rd May 1927, outside the Divisional Headquarters, Pennefather's Road, Aldershot. Lt General Sir Peter Strickland, who commanded the Division in the War, handed over the memorial to his successor, Major General Sir Cecil Romer. (Photo courtesy of the National Army Museum)

Unveiling of the 2nd Division Memorial at the top of Hospital Hill, Aldershot, 1st December 1923. (Photo courtesy of Paul Vickers)

Hugh Hornby, who had served as a Chaplain with the Division from 1915, conducted the service of dedication.

On Queen's Avenue is the "lion" monument in memory of men of the 8th Division who fell in France and Belgium. The 8th Division was one of the new divisions formed in Aldershot during the war. The monument was unveiled by General Sir Francis Davies on Friday 10th April 1924.

For many years the Old Contemptibles, veterans of the British Expeditionary Force of 1914, held their annual parade at the Royal Garrison Church. On 24th August 1958, the 44th Anniversary of the Battle of Mons, the drive leading to the Church was renamed "Old Contemptibles Avenue" in their honour, the ceremony performed by the GOC Aldershot, Major General R. A. Bramwell-Davis.

In 1926 the old Iron Church on Queen's Avenue was demolished and replaced by a new Church

Unveiling of the 8th Division Monument, 1924. (Photo courtesy of Paul Vickers)

of Scotland in memory of the many Scots who gave their lives in the war. St. Andrew's Garrison Church was opened on 10th December 1927 by the Princess Royal. However, shortage of money had meant that it had not been built to the full original plan and it did not have the space for all the Scottish soldiers who wanted to worship there. As a result it was closed in the 1930s for extension work, and re-opened by HM King George VI and Queen Elizabeth on 12th January 1939. Inside is a memorial window to all ranks of 1st Corps who died in the Great War, and a memorial window to Field Marshal Haig.

Aldershot town's municipal war memorial was financed by a public subscription launched by the Mayor in January 1924. The Cornish granite obelisk was unveiled in the Municipal Gardens on the 18th March 1925 by HRH The Duke of Gloucester, in a ceremony attended by huge crowds. A second memorial, the Heroes' Garden, was laid out in Manor Park.

In Farnborough a hospital was opened as a memorial to the dead of the First World War. Situated in Albert Road, this was the Farnborough and Cove Cottage Hospital, and the building is now known as Devereux House.

In addition, may local churches and institutions have memorials to their members and individuals who died in the war.

The Aldershot town war memorial unveiled in Municipal Gardens on the 18th March 1925. (Photo courtesy of Aldershot Military Museum)

Graves of soldiers who died in the First World War, below the Cross of Sacrifice in Aldershot Military Cemetery.
(Photo by Paul Vickers)

APPENDIX

Aldershot Command in August 1914

Aldershot Garrison

North Camp: Marlborough Lines

Lille Barracks: Royal Field Artillery, XXVI Brigade, HQ plus 116, 117 and 118 Batteries. *Strength: 483.*

Blenheim Barracks: 1st Bn, Coldstream Guards. *Strength: 680.*

Malplaquet Barracks: 2nd Bn, Royal Munster Fusiliers. *Strength: 742.*

Oudenarde Barracks: 1st Bn, Black Watch. *Strength: 635.*

Ramillies Barracks: 1st Bn, Scots Guards. *Strength: 685.*

Tournay Barracks: 1st Bn, Loyal North Lancashire Regiment. *Strength: 731.*

South Camp: Stanhope Lines

Gibraltar Barracks: Royal Engineers, A Signal Co, 5, 11 and 23 (Field) Co, 1 and 2 Signal Co, 1 Bridging Train, Training Depot for Field Units, Army Signal School. *Strength: 1,540.*

Albuhera Barracks: 2nd Bn, Oxfordshire and Buckinghamshire Light Infantry. *Strength: 611.*

Barossa Barracks: 2nd Bn, Connaught Rangers. *Strength: 655.*

Corunna Barracks: 2nd Bn, Worcestershire Regiment. *Strength: 618.*

Maida Barracks: 2nd Bn, Highland Light Infantry. *Strength: 605.*

Mandora Barracks: 1st Bn, Royal Berkshire Regiment. *Strength: 787.*

Buller Barracks: Army Service Corps, Horse Transport Companies: 1 (Transport Depot), 7, 9, 10, 16, 20, 26, 27, 28, 31, 35, 36; Mechanical Transport Companies: 52 (MT Depot), 53, 54, 57, 58, 59, 60, 61; Supply Companies: A (Supply Depot), C. *Strength: 1,887.*

McGrigor Barracks: Royal Army Medical Corps, 1, 2 and 3 Companies; A, B and C Depot Companies. *Strength: 958.*

South Camp: Wellington Lines

Badajos Barracks: 2nd Bn, South Staffordshire Regiment. *Strength: 535.*

Salamanca Barracks: 1st Bn, King's Royal Rifle Corps. *Strength: 678.*

Talavera Barracks: 1st Bn, King's (Liverpool) Regiment. *Strength: 814.*

Waterloo Barracks West: Royal Horse Artillery, IV Brigade, J Battery; VII Brigade, I and L Batteries. *Strength: 525.*

Waterloo Barracks East: Royal Field Artillery, XXXIV Brigade, HQ plus 22, 50 and 70 Batteries. *Strength: 451.*

Royal Garrison Artillery, 1st Heavy Brigade, HQ plus 26, 35 and 108 Batteries. *Strength: 432.*

Royal Artillery Mounted Band. *Strength: 61.*

South Camp: Cavalry Barracks

Willems Barracks: 2nd Dragoon Guards. *Strength: 600.*

Warburg Barracks: 5th Dragoon Guards. *Strength: 605.*

Beaumont Barracks: 11th Hussars. *Strength: 656.*

Beaumont Barracks: 15th Hussars (detachment). *Strength: 266.*

Supporting troops

Army Ordnance Corps, Companies 1 and 4. *Strength: 219.*

Military Police, Foot and Mounted. *Strength: 101.*

Army Veterinary Corps, 1 and 2 Sections. *Strength: 61.*

Army Pay Corps. *Strength: 22.*

Total Aldershot Garrison: 17,643

Farnborough

Royal Flying Corps: HQ, Airship Detachment, Kite Section, 1, 5, 6 and 7 Squadrons, Aircraft Park.

Total Farnborough: 564

Bordon

Guadaloupe Barracks: 1st Bn, Royal West Surrey Regiment. *Strength: 707.*

St Lucia Barracks: 1st Bn, South Wales Borderers. *Strength: 610.*

Quebec Barracks: 1st Bn, Gloucestershire Regiment. *Strength: 626.*

Martinique Barracks: 2nd Bn, Welsh Regiment. *Strength: 584.*

Royal Field Artillery, XXIX Brigade, HQ plus 46, 51 and 54 Batteries; XLI Brigade, HQ plus 4, 16 and 17 Batteries. *Strength: 906.*

Royal Engineers, 26 (Field) Co. *Strength: 118.*

Army Service Corps, 13 Co (Horse Transport). *Strength: 101.*

Plus detachments of Royal Army Medical Corps and Army Ordnance Corps. *Strength: 15.*

Total Bordon: *3,667*

Blackdown

Dettingen Barracks: 1st Bn, Northamptonshire Regiment. *Strength: 663.*
Alma Barracks: 2nd Bn, King's Royal Rifle Corps. *Strength: 702.*

Total Blackdown: *1,365*

Ewshott

Royal Field Artillery, XXXVI Brigade, HQ plus 15, 48 and 71 Batteries; XLIV Brigade, HQ plus 47, 56 and 60 Batteries. *Strength: 933.*
Detachments of Royal Army Medical Corps and Army Ordnance Corps. *Strength: 5.*

Total Ewshott: *938*

Deepcut

Royal Field Artillery, XXV Brigade, HQ plus 113, 114 and 115 Batteries; XLIII (Howitzer) Brigade, HQ plus 30, 40 and 57 Batteries.

Total Deepcut: *930*

Pirbright

2nd Bn, Grenadier Guards. *Strength: 735.*
Detachments of Army Service Corps, Royal Army Medical Corps and Army Ordnance Corps. *Strength: 19.*

Total Pirbright: *754*

Woking

Inkerman Barracks: 2nd Bn, Royal Sussex Regiment. *Strength: 722.*
Detachments of Army Service Corps, Royal Army Medical Corps and Army Ordnance Corps. *Strength: 13.*

Total Woking: *735*

Longmoor

15th Hussars. *Strength: 291.*

Royal Engineers, 8 and 10 (Railway) Companies, Railway Depot, 1 Signal Sqn. *Strength: 285.*

Detachments of Army Service Corps, Royal Army Medical Corps and Army Ordnance Corps. *Strength: 11.*

Total Longmoor: 587

Detachments at various stations

Royal Engineers, Army Service Corps, Royal Army Medical Corps, Royal Artillery Clerks' Section, and Royal Engineers Clerks.

Total Various: 62

Total Aldershot Command: 27,245

Information compiled by Paul H. Vickers. Sources:

Army List, August 1914

Distribution of Regimental Strength of the Army, August 1914

Barracks Finder, Aldershot Military Museum website, http://www3.hants.gov.uk/aldershot-museum/local-history-aldershot/barracks.htm

Order of Battle of Divisions, Part 1 - the Regular British Divisions. Official History of the Great War, HMSO 1935